CHIMPANZEES

Please visit our web site at: www.garethstevens.com
For a free color catalog describing Gareth Stevens Publishing's
list of high-quality books and multimedia programs, call
1-800-542-2595 (USA) or 1-800-387-3178 (Canada).
Gareth Stevens Publishing's fax: (414) 332-3567.

Library of Congress Cataloging-in-Publication Data

All about chimpanzees.
    Chimpanzees. — North American ed.
      p. cm. — (All about wild animals)
    Includes index.
    Contents: A closer look — Home, sweet home — Neighbors — The family —
Life in the community — Favorite foods — Danger! — A chimpanzee's day —
Relatives — Humans and chimps.
    ISBN 0-8368-4171-9 (lib. bdg.)
    1. Chimpanzees—Juvenile literature. [1. Chimpanzees.] I. Title. II. Series.
QL737.P96A3625   2004
599.885—dc22   2003063326

This edition first published in 2004 by
Gareth Stevens Publishing
A World Almanac Education Group Company
330 West Olive Street, Suite 100
Milwaukee, Wisconsin 53212 USA

This U.S. edition copyright © 2004 by Gareth Stevens, Inc. Original edition
copyright © 2002 by DeAgostini UK Limited. First published in 2002 as
My Animal Kingdom: All About Chimpanzees by DeAgostini UK Ltd., Griffin House,
161 Hammersmith Road, London W6 8SD, England. Additional end matter
copyright © 2004 by Gareth Stevens, Inc.

Editorial and design: Tucker Slingsby Ltd., London
Gareth Stevens series editor: Catherine Gardner
Gareth Stevens art direction: Tammy Gruenewald

Picture Credits
NHPA — Andy Rouse: cover, title page, 17; Christophe Ratier: 6, 13; Steve
    Robinson: 7, 25, 28; E. A. Janes: 11, 21; Martin Harvey: 14-15, 27, 29;
    Nigel J. Dennis: 16, 25; Anthony Bannister: 20; Gerard Lacz: 28.
Oxford Scientific Films — Clive Bromhall: 8, 17, 18; Mike Birkhead: 9; Nick
    Gordon: 11, 15; Steve Turner: 11, 15; Jen and Des Bartlett: 12; Ronald
    Toms: 12; Stan Osolinski: 13, 20, 21; Richard Packwood: 14, 23; Jackie
    le Fevre: 19; H. S. Terrace: 19; Norbert Rosing: 22; John Downer: 23;
    Michael W. Richards: 24; Martyn Colbeck: 26; Konrad Wothe: 26.

Printed in the United States of America

1 2 3 4 5 6 7 8 9 08 07 06 05 04

ALL about WiLD ANiMaLs

CHIMPANZEES

Gareth Stevens Publishing
A WORLD ALMANAC EDUCATION GROUP COMPANY

CHIMP FACTS

ANIMAL GROUP: mammal

COLOR: dark brown or black

SIZE: Adults are 3 to 5.5 feet (1 to 1.7 meters) tall when they are standing.

WEIGHT: Adult males weigh 75 to 155 pounds (34 to 70 kilograms). Females weigh 55 to 110 pounds (25 to 50 kg).

EATS: mainly leaves and fruit but, sometimes, animals

LIVES: up to 40 years in the wild and up to 60 years in captivity

CONTENTS

Words that appear in the glossary
are printed in **boldface** type the
first time they occur in the text.

A Closer Look

Chimpanzees are a kind of **ape**. They live in Africa and are closely related to gorillas, **gibbons**, and even humans. In fact, chimpanzees, or "chimps," for short, are the wild animals most like humans. Chimps are small compared to some kinds of apes, but they are very strong. Thick, dark hair covers their bodies, except for their faces, ears, hands, and feet. They look cute and cuddly, but chimps can be fierce in the wild.

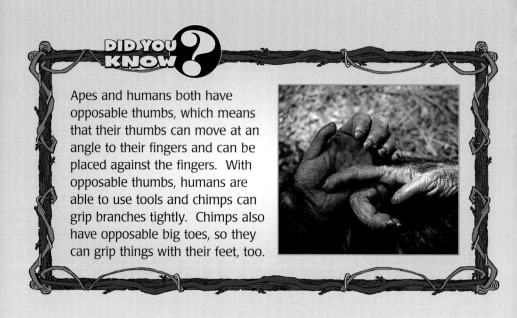

DID YOU KNOW?

Apes and humans both have opposable thumbs, which means that their thumbs can move at an angle to their fingers and can be placed against the fingers. With opposable thumbs, humans are able to use tools and chimps can grip branches tightly. Chimps also have opposable big toes, so they can grip things with their feet, too.

My long, strong fingers and thumbs help me grasp branches and swing through the trees.

I walk on my knuckles instead of on the palms of my hands.

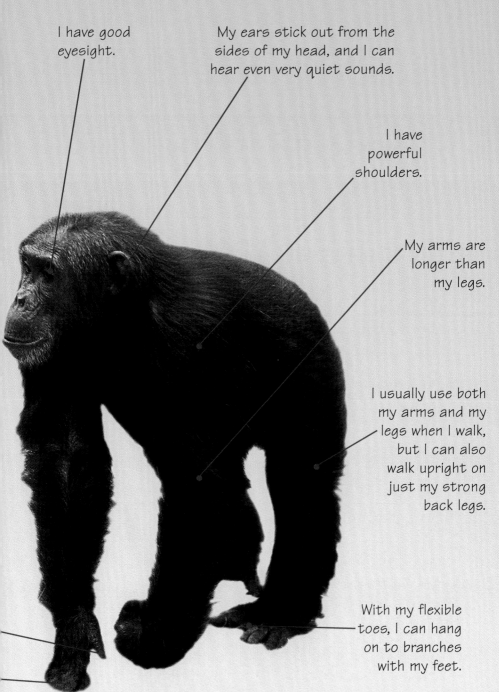

I have good eyesight.

My ears stick out from the sides of my head, and I can hear even very quiet sounds.

I have powerful shoulders.

My arms are longer than my legs.

I usually use both my arms and my legs when I walk, but I can also walk upright on just my strong back legs.

With my flexible toes, I can hang on to branches with my feet.

7

Chimpanzees have round faces with large ears and big jaws. Baby chimps have pink faces, but their faces become darker as they get older. Chimps see and hear very well, and they have big brains. In the wild, they will use rocks, leaves, and other natural objects as hammers, sponges, and even napkins! Scientists have taught them to solve puzzles and to **communicate** with humans, using hand signals.

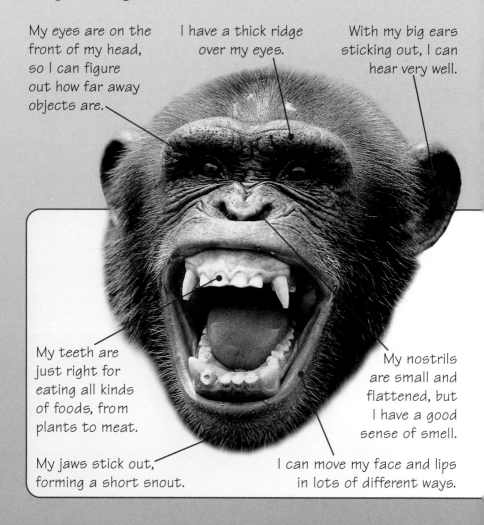

My eyes are on the front of my head, so I can figure out how far away objects are.

I have a thick ridge over my eyes.

With my big ears sticking out, I can hear very well.

My teeth are just right for eating all kinds of foods, from plants to meat.

My jaws stick out, forming a short snout.

My nostrils are small and flattened, but I have a good sense of smell.

I can move my face and lips in lots of different ways.

WALKING TALL

Chimps usually walk on all fours, using their knuckles to support their upper bodies. In this position, they can move at a fast gallop. Chimps can also walk on two legs, the same way humans do. Chimps walk on two legs when they need to carry food or look over tall grass or when they are angry or excited. Chimps climb well, too. They can scamper up trees and swing by their arms from branch to branch. At night, chimps stay in the trees, resting in nests they make out of branches.

FUNNY FACES

Chimps cannot speak, but they can communicate with their voices and their faces. They can make lots of sounds, and the faces they make show how they feel.

afraid

happy

sad

excited

angry

9

HOME, SWEET HOME

Chimps live in wooded areas of western and central Africa. Most chimps prefer to live in dense tropical rain forests that are full of juicy plants to eat, but some chimps live on the edges of the huge African grasslands, called the savanna, or in woodlands that are not as dense as rain forests. To survive, chimps must live near trees that have leaves on them all year long.

A F R

WHERE IN THE WORLD?

Today, apes are found in the wild only in Africa and Asia. Three different kinds of common chimp **species** live in Africa. The western common chimp lives along the western coast. The central common chimp lives in the middle of Africa. The eastern common chimp lives in east-central Africa. Apes, including chimps, and monkeys belong to a group of mammals known as primates. The first primates lived about fifty million years ago and were much smaller than most primates are now. Over a very long time, many primates grew larger, and their brains grew bigger. They began to look more like the apes and monkeys we see today.

LAZING AROUND

The shade of a tree is the perfect place to be during the heat of the day. A group of chimps usually rests after eating. Then the group travels to the next feeding place.

The bonobo, or pygmy chimp, (*right*) is closely related to the common chimp (*below*). Bonobos are shorter and weigh less than the common chimp and have smaller ears and darker faces.

NEIGHBORS

The warm, damp rain forests, where many chimps live, are home to a wide variety of amazing animals. Brightly colored birds and butterflies flutter among the branches. Termites, ants, and hundred of other insects crawl along the leaf-covered ground or fly through the air. Snakes, from tiny tree snakes to giant pythons and cobras, slither along branches and across the forest floor. Antelope and wild pigs hide in the shadows. Monkeys hoot and call to each other, while eagles, leopards, and other hungry **predators** hunt their **prey**.

FOREST GIANTS

Rain forests provide lots of food, so the animals that live there often grow to be extra large. A giant Goliath frog, living in the shelter of the undergrowth, weighs as much as a large house cat. Spiders the size of a child's hand lie in wait for a passing meal, and some millipedes grow to be as long as this open book!

SNAKES ALIVE!

Snakes are hard to see — until they move. A green tree snake, for example, looks like part of its leafy home — until it strikes!

LET'S HIDE!

The bongo, which is a kind of antelope, has stripes on its coat that look like splashes of sunshine against its dark fur. The stripes that seem so bright actually make the bongo harder to see in the flickering shadows of the forest. Many forest animals have light or dark stripes or spots. Stripes and spots hide animals from both their enemies and their prey.

PLAYMATES

Baboons live on the African savanna and in the open woodlands nearby. They eat grass, leaves, birds' eggs, lizards, and baby antelope. Young chimps and baboons sometimes play together, but adult chimpanzees hunt baboons. One difference between a monkey, such as the baboon, and an ape, such as the chimp, is a tail. Monkeys have tails, but apes do not.

THE FAMILY

Chimps live in groups that are called communities. A community has up to eighty members. The members of a community share the same **territory**, but they do not stay together all the time. When the chimps sleep or look for food, they often split up into smaller family groups. Some chimps in a community meet only once in a while. Other chimps are good friends and spend a lot of time playing and **grooming** together. Sometimes, two chimps in a community will fight with each other to determine which one is the most important.

Female chimpanzees typically have one baby at a time, every three or four years. A female chimp usually gives birth to her baby at night — and alone. A baby chimp is helpless. It cannot take care of itself at all. For the first few years, a chimp relies on its mother for food, shelter, and transportation. At first, the baby chimp rides under its mother, clinging to her belly. When it is five or six months old, the young chimp starts to ride on its mother's back.

Baby File

Birth to Four Years

During its first few years of life, a baby chimpanzee stays close to its mother. It drinks her milk, rides on her belly or back, and sleeps with her at night. Little chimps play a lot. Their play often imitates, or copies, adults. By imitating adult chimps, a young chimp learns how to use tools, find food, make a nest, and take its place among the other chimps in the community.

Five to Seven Years

At about four or five years old, a young chimp stops drinking its mother's milk and no longer rides on her back. The chimp starts to do more things on its own, but it still stays close to its mother until it is about seven years old.

Eight to Ten Years

After the age of seven, a young female chimp still lives near her mother and learns how to take care of babies. A young male chimp will start spending more time with adult males. At the age of eight or nine, a chimp can survive on its own.

LIFE IN THE COMMUNITY

Chimpanzees communicate with the other chimps in the community in many different ways. They send messages by making different faces and by holding their bodies in different positions. Chimps greet each other, for example, with hugs, pats, and kisses. Although chimps do not speak words, they can grunt, whistle, and hoot. When a chimp sees danger, it warns the community by making a loud, wailing sound. Resting chimps grunt softly to each other. Young chimps laugh as they play together.

WATCH OUT!

When a male chimp is angry, he shows it! He walks on two legs, swaying from side to side in a threatening way. His hair bristles, and with an ugly scowl on his face, he waves his arms around and, sometimes, screams loudly. The chimp may even throw rocks or branches. All of the other chimps in the group know that these signs mean they should stay away.

DINNERTIME

When a chimp finds food, it gives a loud call followed by a scream. This sound is called a pant-hoot. A pant-hoot invites all the other chimps in the community to join the caller for a good meal. Each chimp has its own pant-hoot so the whole community will know which member of the group is calling.

HAND SIGNALS

Besides studying the way chimpanzees communicate with each other in the wild, scientists have also taught some chimps to communicate using the same sign language deaf people use. A young chimp called Washoe learned more than three hundred signs. Then, she started making up her own signs for words she did not know!

FAVORITE FOODS

Chimpanzees spend seven or eight hours a day looking for food and eating. Most often, they eat parts of plants, including leaves, seeds, and fruits. Chimps also eat ants, **termites**, birds and their eggs, and small **rodents**. They sometimes even hunt young monkeys and deer. Chimps make and use tools more than any other animal, and many of their tools help them gather or eat food. They break open tough nuts by pounding them with rocks, and they use small sticks to catch ants and termites.

TASTY TERMITES

Chimps like to eat termites, and a good way to catch termites is to fish for them. A chimp will dip a stem of grass or a thin twig into a termite nest, wait for the insects to crawl onto it, then pull out the termite-covered stem or twig for a tasty treat.

MEATY MEAL

Chimps will sometimes form a small group to hunt monkeys, such as baby colobus monkeys or baboons. The group's leader feeds first, then calls the other chimps in the group to join the feast. Chimps chew meat slowly, and they often chew up a bunch of leaves at the same time.

JUICY FOOD

Chimpanzees get most of the water they need from the juicy foods they eat. When chimps do need a drink, however, they dip their hands into water and lick off the drops. Chimps will also crush wet leaves and squeeze the water into their mouths as if they were squeezing it out of a sponge.

DANGER!

Adult chimpanzees do not have many enemies, but young chimps are easy prey for hungry hunters. Leopards, lions, large eagles, or baboons will snatch young chimps when they are not close to their mothers. Sometimes, adult chimps fight and kill other adult chimps from different territories. Chimps also die from diseases and falls from tree branches. Human hunters, however, may be a chimp's greatest enemies. People hunt and kill chimps for meat. They also capture and sell chimps to zoos and collectors.

SILENT HUNTER

A leopard hunts at dawn or dusk, when its spotted coat blends in with the patchy shadows of the rain forest or savanna. Sometimes, the leopard waits silently on a tree branch and leaps down when its prey walks by. At other times, the leopard quietly **stalks** its prey. When it gets close enough, it **pounces**, then kills its victim with one quick bite. A baby chimp is a tasty snack for a hungry leopard.

TERRIBLE TALONS

The crowned hawk eagle usually hunts monkeys, but a young chimp without its mother makes a nice meal, too. The sharp-eyed eagle sits patiently on a tree branch. When a young chimp comes close, the eagle swoops down, grabs the chimp in its talons, and flies off to find a safe place to eat.

BUSHMEAT

The **scrub** and forest areas of Africa are called "the bush," and the animals killed there for food are known as "bushmeat." Although hunting chimpanzees is illegal, many people do it anyway. For some of the local people, hunting chimps and other wild animals is their main source of food. For wealthy people, however, bushmeat is a **delicacy**, and they will pay a lot of money to serve it.

A Chimpanzee's Day

5:00 AM
As the Sun began to rise, I stretched. I heard leaves rustle as other chimps started waking up, too. I fed my baby my milk and groomed her by picking the dirt and **parasites** out of her hair.

6:00 AM
My six-year-old joined us. She is too old, now, to sleep with me. She sleeps in her own nest but stays near me during the day. She still has lots to learn. We groomed each other before we started our day.

7:00 AM
I heard the calls of the other chimps in the community. They were getting ready to look for food. The baby rode on my back as we moved through the forest.

10:00 AM
We found a fig tree full of ripe fruit, so we had a good meal. Then, we rested in a clearing. The youngest chimps in our group ran around, playing and tickling each other.

12:00 NOON
We heard a loud, sudden sound. A big male chimp ran out from among the trees and started jumping around, throwing rocks, and breaking off branches. After showing us he was the boss, he settled down to eat.

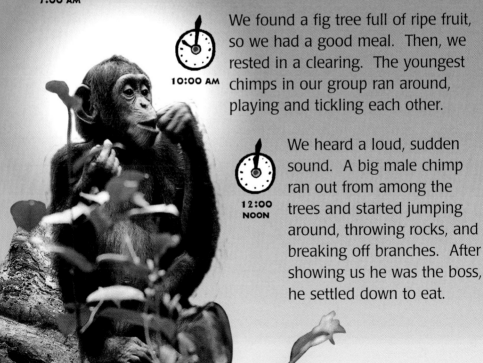

2:00 PM

I poked a twig into a termite nest. When the termites crawled onto the twig, I pulled it out, and my youngsters got a snack — as well as a hunting lesson.

4:00 PM

Searching for our last big meal of the day, we found a bush covered with delicious berries. What a treat!

6:00 PM

As night approached, I climbed a nearby tree. I chose two strong branches for a nest and bent smaller branches over them. I lined the nest with leafy twigs.

7:00 PM

The pant-hoot of a male chimp echoed through the forest. Other chimps added their own sounds as we settled down to sleep.

2:00 AM

A loud screech woke us up and frightened my baby. I groomed the baby and let her drink some of my milk before I put her back down to sleep.

4:00 AM

It will soon be dawn. The forest is still quiet, so I think I'll snuggle up and snooze for a few more minutes.

25

RELATIVES

Chimpanzees are one of many kinds of apes. The smallest kinds of apes, which are known as lesser apes, include all of the different species of gibbons. The largest kinds of apes, called great apes, include gorillas, orangutans, chimpanzees, and bonobos, or pygmy chimps. Bonobos are the common chimp's closest relatives. Bonobos live only in the forests of Zaire, which is a country in central Africa.

GREAT APE OF THE FOREST

The orange orangutan looks very human for an animal. At about 3 feet (1 meter) tall, it is the world's largest tree-dwelling animal. Full-grown male orangutans have big cheek pouches. When two males meet, they puff out their cheeks, which makes them look very scary. The orangutan lives only in Asia.

GENTLE GIANT

Like chimps, gorillas are from Africa. In the wild, they live in groups led by a head male, which is called a silverback. A full-grown male gorilla is about as tall as an adult man but more than twice as heavy — and very strong! These great apes look fierce, but they are actually shy **herbivores**.

DID YOU KNOW?

• Chimpanzees are the animal species most closely related to humans, and chimps can catch many of the same illnesses that humans catch.

• Unlike any other animals, except humans, chimps can recognize themselves in mirrors.

Humans and Chimps

Chimps are known by humans around the world. They appear in zoos, circuses, and even movies. Cute, cuddly, and funny, chimpanzees often look almost like small children, and some people try to keep them as pets.

Humans are a threat to chimps. Wild chimpanzees are caught and sold as pets or performers, and they are so much like humans that scientists use them to find out more about human diseases. Humans also hunt chimps for food and destroy their homes.

Cute and Clever

Chimps were first brought to Europe from Africa more than three hundred years ago. The animals looked cute, and they learned tricks quickly. Ever since then, humans have kept chimpanzees as pets and have trained them as performers for movies and circuses.

A Good Friend

Jane Goodall studied chimps in Africa's Gombe National Park for more than forty years. She carefully watched the chimps and helped people understand how chimpanzees live.

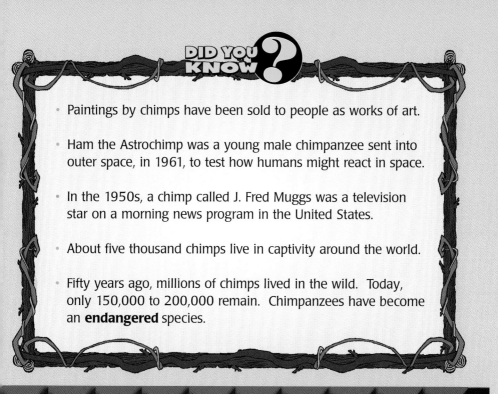

- Paintings by chimps have been sold to people as works of art.

- Ham the Astrochimp was a young male chimpanzee sent into outer space, in 1961, to test how humans might react in space.

- In the 1950s, a chimp called J. Fred Muggs was a television star on a morning news program in the United States.

- About five thousand chimps live in captivity around the world.

- Fifty years ago, millions of chimps lived in the wild. Today, only 150,000 to 200,000 remain. Chimpanzees have become an **endangered** species.

SAVE THE CHIMPS

In West Africa, chimps are very rare because most of the trees in their forest homes have been cut down to make room for farmland. Logging companies are moving into new areas of the rain forests to cut down trees for lumber, which is used all over the world

to build homes and furniture. When people cut down trees, however, they also destroy the homes of chimpanzees and other animals, making it easier for people to capture or kill the animals. Some people are trying to save wild chimps by working with African governments to set aside land for national parks, where chimps can live in safety.

Glossary

APE

A long-armed animal with a hairy body and grasping fingers and toes, but no tail, which belongs to the group of mammals that look the most like humans and are the most intelligent next to humans.

COMMUNICATE

To share information using sounds, signs or symbols, or body positions and movements.

DELICACY

A rare or unusual food that is considered a luxury to eat.

ENDANGERED

At risk of dying out as a species.

GIBBONS

The smallest kinds of apes, which live mainly in Southeast Asia.

GROOMING

Taking care of the body, especially the hair, to remove any kind of dirt and to make it neat and attractive.

HERBIVORES

Animals that eat only plants.

PARASITES

Animals or plants that survive by living and feeding on or inside of another animal or plant.

POUNCES

Jumps on top of something suddenly and unexpectedly.

PREDATORS
Animals that hunt other animals for food.

PREY
Animals that another animal hunts and kills for food.

RODENTS
Mammals, such as mice, rats, and squirrels, that have large, sharp front teeth, which are used for gnawing.

SCRUB
An area of land that is usually very dry and has only low shrubs and small trees growing on it.

SPECIES
Groups of animals in which members of a group have many of the same physical features and behaviors and can mate with each other to produce offspring.

STALKS
Hunts or tracks in a slow, quiet, secretive way.

TERMITES
Insects that live in colonies, in large mounds of earth, and feed on wood, often destroying wooden structures.

TERRITORY
A large area of land claimed by someone or something for a particular use.

INDEX